DAMAGED

*A First Responder's Experiences
Handling Post-Traumatic Stress Disorder*

JAMES MEUER

WestBow
PRESS
A DIVISION OF THOMAS NELSON

"Bridge of Fear" used with permission, written by Tracy Castelli.
Chapter heading artwork drawn by Jordan Meuer.
Author photo and other artwork was done by Nick Castelli.

WestBow Press books may be ordered through booksellers or by contacting:

WestBow Press
A Division of Thomas Nelson
1663 Liberty Drive
Bloomington, IN 47403
www.westbowpress.com
1-(866) 928-1240

ISBN: 978-1-4497-9955-7 (sc)
ISBN: 978-1-4497-9956-4 (e)

Library of Congress Control Number: 2013911506

Printed in the United States of America.

WestBow Press rev. date: 06/25/2013

DEDICATED TO

Sara—my Princess
Jordan—Baby Girl
Christopher—Batman Jr.
Daniel—you're not forgotten
And to all first responders everywhere.

Thanks to the Lord for rescuing me, to Tracy for believing in
and always encouraging me, and to Dad and Mom
for giving me life.

FOREWORD

You met him a long time ago. He tried not acknowledging your existence, but deep down he knew you were there. Like emptiness in the pit of his stomach, you settled in, slowly at first. You began to mold him into something he's not. At first he didn't realize the change, but you knew what you were doing. When he did acknowledge you, you lied to him. He believed the lies that he wasn't good enough, didn't do enough, and just wasn't enough of a man. He started to believe the lies almost to his own detriment. Noises, voices, and emotional distress were your homework. He tried so hard to avoid you, but you wouldn't have it. You imprisoned him in his own mind. He wasn't safe anywhere, according to you. He is strong but couldn't fight this alone. It wasn't until he held up his hands to the Lord that God sent someone to hold his hands up for him. He became stronger and stronger. Is he saved from you? Absolutely, yes! Will you leave him alone? I don't think for a moment that you will. But his God is greater than you and will have victory in his life.

In Christ, he is loved, cherished, and valuable. He is a leader in this life and will persevere. God will have his way with James. PTSD (Post-Traumatic Stress Disorder)—you are just letters of the alphabet.

Written by Tracy Castelli (the love of my life)

ACKNOWLEDGEMENTS

Writing this was like poking a hornet's nest with a stick. It stirred up a lot of emotions that had been long repressed, some since the time of the incidents detailed. Every call I talk about is real. All identifiers (names, dates, etc.), except for Tracy and myself, have been changed.

There is no possible way to tell every story that has affected me. These few barely scratch the surface. Sharing my experiences is my way of crying with others in pain. I'm not the only one who lived through these incidents. I have a lot of gratitude for the partners I had through all my years (you know who you are). I was a paramedic for twenty-six years, and all but a few were spent working in the 911 system. There are many other medics and first responders, not unlike myself, that I'm hoping to reach out to offer some reassurance, to let them know they aren't alone and that it's okay to feel. It's even okay to cry. Depression, anxiety, and panic attacks aren't a sign of weakness, they are signs of having tried to remain strong for too long. Throwing away chaos, drama, and the things hurled at us must be deliberate, for it is in doing so that we find freedom, compassion, clarity, and a place where our hearts are no longer atrophied but are open to living the life we were meant to live. This is for all the men and women who do the job, don't get paid what they're worth, and give their heart and soul to people they don't know. Yesterday is over. We can't go back and redo anything that has happened . . . regret nothing that once made you happy.

> Greater love has no one than this, that he
> lay down his life for his friends.
> —John 15:13 (New International Version)

CHAPTER 1

"Memorial Hospital, medic forty-two, we are code four, 10-55," I said into the radio.

"What does he mean she's dead? She's a kid—why isn't he doing anything?" I heard the doctor bark in the background.

Was he right? Why didn't I do something—anything?

The nurse interrupted. "Dr. Bryant, I know this medic, I trust his—"

I'd had enough, so I blurted, "Tell the doc the girl's brain is on the road, and last I checked, that's a separation of vital body organs!"

The following radio silence seemed to last forever. I hated doctors. They just didn't seem to think we paramedics knew what we were doing out there. And to think I went to school to be a doctor.

"Copy, medic forty-two," was all I heard.

We usually worked on children until all efforts were exhausted. This wasn't going to happen for this little girl. She had turned seven just a month earlier. Today, as she left for school, the simple act of walking across the street in front of her house in a new residential area, with very little traffic (or more likely no traffic) ended any dreams she may have had—and started me on a downward spiral trying to forget. It wasn't her fault. After all, I "didn't even try to save her."

I was standing there staring, taking it all in, yet I was spinning. It was not a dizzy spinning but the kind where you are actually

1

turning around in circles. But I was standing still. People came out in a swarm, like fire ants after you kick the anthill. An older man wearing a bathrobe came up with a camera around his neck. I had placed a yellow emergency blanket over the girl, and he wanted me to pull it back so he could take pictures.

"Get out of here! Geez, this is nothing you need to be taking pictures of," I responded, curt and tense.

"The pictures ain't for me, they are for the family," he retorted.

"Are you kidding me? You really think they want pictures of this? Get out of here!" I said with angry authority.

Again, the words were out before I could stop them. He needed to go away! Suddenly there was a cacophony of sounds. I heard talking all around me, but I couldn't make out what anyone was saying. I was searching the crowd to find who was talking. They were all talking. My partner put his hand on my shoulder.

"I'm gonna tell the school bus driver. You go tell the girl's mom."

"What? Okay." I was startled.

What would I say? How do you tell a mother her precious little girl was run over by a school bus and is now dead in front of her house? The scene seemed to spin around me. I was hearing an overwhelming amount of noise, as if a hundred people were standing around on the sidewalk behind the yellow tape. The CHP (California Highway Patrol) officers were looking at the yellow blanket covering the little girl. The sun had only been up a few hours. I was sweating even as a cool morning breeze touched me.

"Did you hear me?" my partner asked, snapping me back to the reality of what was going on around me.

"Yeah, where's her mom?" I quietly responded.

"Check the house," he said over his shoulder as he walked to the school bus parked down the street.

The bus had continued to the end of the street after hitting her, only stopping after someone forced the driver to stop. She didn't know what had happened at her last stop and continued driving to the school. The driver had stopped across the street from the little girl's house. The children filed on to the bus. After waiting a few minutes, she closed the doors and headed to the school. A moment later, a car with a frantic driver honking the horn pulled up alongside the bus at the corner stop sign. Words were exchanged. The driver screamed. That was her last day as a bus driver. She had already written out a resignation letter and was handing it to the school officials at the same time I found the little girl's mother.

As I was walking up the driveway, the girl's mother was coming toward me. I was surprised by her calmness. Her face was serene. I thought she would be inconsolable. After all, isn't that the way it's shown on television? Others were approaching, friends or neighbors, I guessed. This woman was about to get the worst news of her life, and I had to deliver it.

"Ma'am, my name is James. I'm a paramedic," I said as my stomach turned. "Ma'am, your daughter—" I started.

I didn't get a chance to say any more before she reached out and took my hand. "Okay," she said quietly and with a calm voice.

She was at peace. Some would say she was in shock. Others might say she didn't care. After all, if she cared, she would have been beside herself, sobbing uncontrollably. She did care. I could see it in her eyes. Those eyes—I'll never forget them. I was drawn into those dark brown eyes. I could see her pain. I felt I caused that pain. Her tragedy became mine; I had to turn to walk away, feeling a twinge of relief and guilt. I felt guilty because I couldn't do anything for her daughter.

An officer was standing by the yellow blanket. "Hey, can you come here?" he queried.

"Uh, yeah, whatcha need?" I asked.

3

"Can you uncover the body so the investigator can take some pictures?" he asked.

I agreed and knelt down to hold up the blanket. There I was staring at her. I was studying the destruction. She had suffered a devastating head injury. There was no other trauma to her little body. Her backpack was still in place, not a speck of dirt on her white shorts or the turquoise shirt she was wearing. Her socks were rolled down to her brand-new shoes. Her shoes—they were white as snow. I wondered how there could not have been a single mark anywhere else on her body. As I stared longer, I didn't realize what I was doing to myself. I wanted to know how this could happen. I thought it had to be the inside rear tire that did the damage. It's the only way. Otherwise there would have been more trauma. The whole scene was seared into my brain. It hurt.

We usually refer to the victims by a description of the trauma or the scene, never by a name. That way we keep them at arm's length. That's how we are supposed to get beyond the horror we see. That way, they don't seem like people who can break our hearts. This little girl had a name. She was Carrie. She was a real person. I couldn't keep her at arm's length. I took her in my arms and held tight. She broke my heart.

I was interrupted. "Did you hear me?" the CHP officer asked.

"Huh? What?" I was startled back to reality.

"I'm all done here. You can cover her back up now," he said.

"What? Yeah, okay," I managed to get out.

Drained, I sat in the passenger front seat of the ambulance and radioed the hospital to inform them of the girl's demise. I was sitting in silence when we were dispatched to another nearby call. We asked to be taken out of service but instead were denied the request and told to take the call. The rest of the shift was clouded. I remember it was extremely busy, and I felt *damaged*.

CHAPTER 2

What I did that day was all wrong—not to Carrie or her mother, but to myself. I didn't know nor would I know for years after this one call the damage I had done to myself. Some things you can only learn by doing the job. No one told me not to think too much about the people. No one told me not to overanalyze the situation.

I sat there that day looking, staring, and engraving in my brain the entire scene. Now, twenty-four years later, I still remember everything about the call. I remember, and I see Carrie lying there, the clothes she was wearing, the backpack still on her back, and her injuries.

I'm not over it. The counselors diagnosed me with PTSD (post-traumatic stress disorder), a severe anxiety disorder that can develop after exposure to any event that results in psychological trauma.

It has loosened its grip on me somewhat. I'm not totally free of being ambushed by the dreams and flashbacks. As I sit here writing this morning, I'm tired from a night of little sleep. The dreams and faces came to me just last night. I tried, for the first time, to make peace with them, without success.

For two years prior to starting this writing, I hadn't slept well. I was plagued by dreams. More often they were dreams of Carrie lying in the street. Her eyes would open, and she would say, "Why didn't you save me?" while she was trying to stand.

The other most common dream was of another little girl I treated who had suffered trauma to one of her eyes. I would feel this tugging on my shirt sleeve and hear her say, "Mister, will my eye grow back?"

On occasion the dreams would be of some other person I had treated, or I would simply be tormented by people screaming or other sights and sounds of my years as a paramedic. This would go on for about seven or eight nights, and then I would get one good night's sleep. I am now able to sleep well most nights only with the help of medication. I still have a rough night every now and again.

It had been more than two years since I left the house except for the occasional doctor's appointment or to attend church. My doctor's office and church were near my home, so I didn't have to be out long. I isolated myself for two years with the thought that it was for the best. It would minimize my exposure to the outside world I had come to fear and to other people.

I had become content with the idea of never having to leave the house. With the Internet I could order anything I needed, have it delivered, and never have to leave my safe zone. The safe zone was that place I created where I felt I could control my immediate environment. If I were to leave for another reason I'd have to be prepared, knowing well in advance where and when I was going and how long I'd be out. I don't do well having to leave on short notice.

I become very anxious to be out in public, driving, shopping, or going to a restaurant. It's even worse if have to go out on my own. My home is my safe zone, and I find myself racing back to it after any trip. The longer I'm away from my safe zone the worse the anxiety becomes. I limit my time outside because in my mind's eye, I see accidents and injuries everywhere and don't want to have a flashback in public.

I really don't know what the trigger (something that has happened that sticks in the mind) will be—a word spoken in a certain tone, a sight my brain recognizes even before I do, or a look from a stranger on the street. Unexpectedly, a synapse will flash and they, the flashbacks, are upon me. My eyes see something and my brain recognizes a site, a street, or a field. Neither my eyes or brain would tell me, but I would respond with fear, anxiety, and utter dread. It seems almost instinctual, like self-preservation.

A trigger may not be obvious at the time it occurs. My mind would be busy dealing with the situation at hand and repress the trigger. Ideally, it should be dealt with soon after it occurs. Many times, though, triggers that aren't dealt with accumulate. Over a long period of time, they can affect judgment, mind-set, and emotions. They take me back to calls I thought I had long forgotten with all the sights, sounds, and smells. It's as if I am doing it over again for the first time and not just simply remembering the call. Those images are imprinted on my subconscious. I see bodies when I go by certain locations if I allow it to happen, and the images of the scene that I had responded to at that location come to mind. They are intense and frightening. And they are real. I also know I'm not alone, and neither are you.

What makes one person last years in his chosen field while another lasts only one day? Some will quit after a day, or less, while others last until retirement. What makes one person "burn out" while someone else, under the same circumstances, thrives? Do they really thrive? Or are they harboring a "thief"? PTSD will steal your sleep, your memories, and your life. PTSD symptoms are caused by witnessing or participating in a traumatic event. Studies also show that people with PTSD can manifest the condition in many ways, both in symptoms and severity. Some might be mildly affected while others can become incapacitated.

We carry the images and memories of every trauma we've encountered since our first day on the job. It can affect two people standing side by side differently. PTSD is rarely cured; it can be treated. While it has been solely used in reference to those in the military suffering with the condition, it is now being recognized in first responders, appropriately named because they are the first to respond to the scene of an emergency. They include paramedics, firefighters, and police officers.

PTSD is a physiological response to noticeably abnormal situations. It involves specific chemical changes in the brain that occur in response to experiencing a traumatic event. Many of the PTSD symptoms appear as a direct result of these brain changes. It is a medical disorder that sometimes causes serious disability. Those with PTSD often have severe mood swings, exhibit antisocial behavior, and may develop substance abuse disorders. In addition they might have significant difficulty at their job, in personal relationships, and with other social activities. They find themselves shopping at two in the morning to avoid crowds. They will choose a seat in a restaurant that has a view of the door.

Family and friends often don't understand. They don't understand the angry outbursts or the episodes of isolation and being quiet. Let me add, if you're reading this and know someone experiencing these signs, please don't take his or her behavior personally, and don't react with anger or frustration. The person may not even know what is happening or what can be done to help.

Do not expect them to just step back in where they left off. They just won't be able to do that. They are still the people you loved before, but they have changed also. They have seen too much of the darker side of life. Like coming in from the dark into light, they too have to adjust to coming back into the world they once knew, the same world that to them is now a scary place. Responding with patience and understanding is very comforting to that person. In my experience, this is the number-one thing that can be done to help. Then find a counselor or ask your church pastor for help.

I assure you that someone experiencing PTSD would rather not be, and it's not in their control. Most people have probably been through frightening experiences and might have symptoms similar to those of PTSD as a result but they do not have the severity of symptoms or the impairment associated with it. The specific brain changes seen in PTSD differ from those seen in a more common form of anxiety. Similarly, the experiences of the common form of anxiety and PTSD are noticeably different.

Personally—and this is my opinion only—I am not of the mind-set that simply witnessing a single event or being in a motor vehicle accident automatically leads to PTSD. A person in those situations, however traumatic to him or her, may be shaken and have some level of anxiety, and the person may even have a bad dream or two, but not to the same degree that leads to PTSD.

I'm not downplaying the feelings and emotions of others. Witnessing an assault or a shooting or being in an accident is emotionally draining and traumatic to the person but doesn't compare to what someone with PTSD has witnessed or been involved. I don't want people thinking or being told they have PTSD simply because they experienced an event. PTSD is ongoing and debilitating. Please don't mistake my opinion as being heartless. I was and still am willing to lay down my life for you, not unlike many other men and women. I don't want PTSD to become an excuse for people to use and as a result detract from the significant disability of those who are truly suffering. PTSD is a complicated disorder with many criteria for diagnosis. The material here is for informational purposes only. I am by no means an authority on PTSD. Seek assistance if you feel that you or your loved one may be suffering from PTSD.

I felt invincible when I put on the uniform. I had been well trained. I had all the tools I needed. What happened next I could never imagine.

CHAPTER 3

I forced the accident with the little girl, Carrie, behind locked doors in my mind. I continued working, trying not to show the deep hurt I felt inside. Every so often I would break and allow myself to cry, but only when I felt it was safe to do so. I tried to talk to my wife when I got home that day; she had no time to listen to me crying about "some little girl." I didn't understand why; she had always listened previously. What I didn't know then was that she had become tired of my job. I was alone. I spent the next four days in seclusion. Until one day in the shower, sobbing uncontrollably, I pushed it all away. It physically hurt my head.

A year later, working the same unit, same zone of our coverage area, same time of morning, and two weeks before Christmas, my partner and I were called to a house fire. We had a brand new EMT (emergency medical technician) student riding with us that day, and she was about to be introduced to EMS (emergency medical services) in one of the worse possible ways. I had never heard such panic over the radio. Halfway there a firefighter was frantic in his request for a second ambulance. The only information we were given was that somebody had been burned. That turned out to be an understatement.

We arrived to find that the fire had been extinguished. There was smoke still billowing out the broken front window. The scene was one of organized chaos. As we were getting our equipment out of the ambulance a firefighter rushed over, grabbed one of the bags, and took off in a sprint. He was shouting something as he disappeared behind one of the fire engines. I took in the scene as we followed. I came around the back of the engine and stopped. I think I cursed, but I'm not sure. I wasn't prepared to see three burned babies lying in a row on a tarp. Then everything went quiet.

The firefighters had found three boys, ages three, four, and five, in the bedroom closet. They said the oldest was huddled over the other two as if he was protecting them from the inferno. Now the three of them lay before me on the ground. There is no way to describe the horror of the burns. They weren't recognizable as children. The burns were extensive and covered their entire bodies. The stench was overwhelming. The firefighter said the two smaller children were breathing when they found them. I didn't know how it was possible. I knew it wasn't, but hearing that they were still breathing just moments before that gave me hope. I always hoped everyone would live. In an instant, the noise of the scene returned like I was punched in the gut. I processed what needed to be done.

I made the decision that nothing could be done for the older boy. He was in the "pugilist" position—if a person is alive but unconscious before getting burned, the burned body will assume a posture similar to that of a boxer in the ring: the arms are raised up as if in a defensive position, and the hands are tightened into fists. The legs may be bent into a defensive stance and the head pulled back as well, almost the opposite of the fetal position. This is due to the contraction of the bigger, stronger muscles as they are burned. His action to cover the younger boys gave them a chance to survive, however small.

The younger boys were still flexible. I directed the EMT student to start CPR on the two younger children while my partner attended to a woman with smoke inhalation. I intubated one boy and then the other. As I passed the tube into their tracheas, I saw no burns in their airways. That was a good sign as it meant they hadn't inhaled super-heated air or smoke. I was relieved.

I asked the fire captain to get a helicopter to transport one of the boys. After it landed I watched as the flight nurse came running toward me. She stopped a few feet away and dropped her bags. I will never forget the look of total shock on her face. I just wanted to say, "Yeah, I know, pretty bad, now get over here!" Instead I went back to focusing on what needed to be done.

So much was going on around me. The second ambulance had arrived at this point. The woman with smoke inhalation was being cared for by that crew. The helicopter took the youngest boy, and I was getting the four-year-old ready for transport.

We loaded the gurney with the boy into the ambulance. As I jumped in the back I remember my partner asking me how I wanted him to get to the trauma/burn center. There were a couple routes he could have taken.

I told him, "I don't care; just get us there."

This was the wrong thing to say to someone who races motorcycles on his days off. During the ride I was trying to start an IV. The boy's skin kept sloughing, making it difficult to get any IV established. The odor of burnt flesh was overpowering. I badly wanted to transfer care of the boy to the doctors and nurses at the hospital.

We made it to the hospital in eleven minutes. This was flying considering the distance.

After I transferred care to the ER, I called my wife. She told me, "I don't want to hear about it. I really don't care." Then she hung up. I walked outside. At this point she had had enough and so had I.

The shift supervisor approached me as I exited the ER doors. He didn't ask if we were okay, how the call went, or exactly what had happened. Instead, he chastised us for driving too fast. I just walked past him, lit a cigarette, and started mentally processing the call. It's hard to wrap your head around seeing three babies burned so badly. It would be hard to imagine one burned baby. I hadn't learned a lesson from the incident with Carrie. Once again I thought about every aspect of the call, trying to figure out how the babies came to be in the closet. With the information I received from the fire department and what I learned on scene, I concluded that the fire had started in the bedroom with the closet where the boys were found. The woman with smoke inhalation was their mother. She had gone across the street, leaving the three boys alone in the house. There was some question as to whether she was involved in recreational drug use, how long she had been absent from the home that morning, and if she truly tried to get the boys out of the house after the fire started. She had told the investigating officers she had attempted to enter the home, only to be pushed back by the heat and flames and thus inhaling smoke. I wasn't the only one to think she wasn't totally truthful. Whatever the truth was, I tried not to care. My supervisor took us out of service and told us to return to the office for something new called CISD (Critical Incident Stress Debriefing).

CISD was something new the company was trying. It was the latest rage in EMS. I didn't believe it was; I had no need for it. After all, how would talking about a call with other medics really help?

We entered the conference room at the main office. I threw my uniform shirt, tainted with the odor of burnt flesh, into the trash and lit a cigarette. My supervisor looked at me, perplexed.

I looked back at him and said one word: "Ashtray." I was indignant. I knew I wasn't allowed to smoke in the building. I didn't care. At this point nothing mattered.

The EMT student quit right there. She said she wasn't cut out for EMS. My partner said he was good. I let out a firestorm of curses, and then I asked for a new shirt so I could get back to work. I had no time for this; it wouldn't help anyway.

I spent time during the rest of the shift thinking about my wife not wanting to listen. I turned to her for comfort and understanding and was denied. Maybe it was because she saw so many changes in me that I hadn't seen. At the time I wasn't aware I had been acting different and that I had changed. We separated two weeks later. It was three days after Christmas. Two months later I was served divorce papers.

CHAPTER 4

Sometimes my family and friends and anyone else who is standing by me find me difficult due to my demeanor and behavior. Sometimes I get tired of explaining to people who don't even care to understand. To speak directly from my experiences gives me a sense of direction.

I have discovered a few things over the years while dealing with my PTSD. While it has taken years to gain this insight, there's still so much more to learn, but this is a start. It is against my nature to talk deeply and personally about this part of my life. I still find it difficult to express these things openly. I know I have issues, but I still find it hard to admit. With this knowledge and insight I hope to make it easier to interact with and help others. Love, support, and encouragement are more helpful than anything else I have found.

Trauma has completely changed me. Who I truly am is still there. It's inside me and really wants to be seen. I became disconnected from my true self. Due to these traumatic events, my real self withdrew, and in order to keep safe, a different personality (not to be confused with multiple personality disorder) emerged like a mask I can't remove. This other self protects me by being ever-vigilant. It keeps me from going outside, it takes a seat in a restaurant so I can see the door, and it is always standing guard while the real me cries in silence, jumps at every noise, and endures the flashbacks and memories. So many times I just want to scream, "I'm still here. Can't you see me?" There's a chance that every now and then I'm going to behave in a manner others perceive as strange. I want so badly to be who I once was. I know I'm still me even if others can't see it.

I didn't see that my life had spun out of control. I wanted to believe my life would return to the way it was, that I could be like I was before. Unfortunately, trauma left a deep scar inside me and returning to "normal" was not likely. It wasn't possible for me to live through traumatic events and be the same. I wasn't aware of the impact doing the job I love would have on me. Still, today I would do it all over even if it meant the same result. My life never returned to the way it was before my experiences. I couldn't go back to the way it was. My past was history, which is good since the new me wouldn't be able to live that life.

The most difficult thing to accept is the reality of living with PTSD. It can make me feel isolated. I had to get used to a new way of thinking and new patterns of behavior. The scars remain and remind us of where we've been, but they don't have to dictate where we're going. Hidden scars are just as real and just as painful. And it's hard to live comfortably with hidden scars.

PTSD changed how I view myself and the world. My self-esteem is shattered, and I feel that I can't rely on myself. In a way, I don't trust my thought processes. They tend to be erratic at times and driven by fear. Therefore, I don't always think straight. This makes it difficult for me to accept the advice and guidance of others because I think they don't understand PTSD enough, or at all, to be able to help me.

My view of the world changed from how it was before the traumatic event. It became a dangerous, unpredictable, and threatening place. I can't go out and do the things I once did. Going out to dinner is frightening. The idea of being around other people in a crowded restaurant is sheer terror. I dread a simple trip to the grocery store. As I mentioned earlier, I see accidents and injuries ready to happen everywhere, which causes extreme anxiety. The faces of people I see all look like patients

I treated. If I do have to go out of the house I plan my routes, make the trip as short as possible, and then rush to get home to my safe zone.

I have spent large amounts of time trying to understand flashbacks and their triggers and reading up on the psychological and physical response to a traumatic event. I attempt to notice what triggers a flashback with the thought that if I know what caused them, it would be easier for me to avoid having one. I became aware of just a few triggers, but in reality I never know when they will happen. The biggest trigger I have is driving in traffic. I'm a cautious driver but others aren't as much. Having someone tailgate me scares me and set in motion a series of automobile accident flashbacks.

I also became aware of the power of a simple touch. The touch of the hand will bring me out of a flashback. While I find it difficult to ask for help, I looked for available treatment options. At this time I haven't found any treatment specific to first responders. The counseling I have gone through seems to be the usual generic psychological material. It has been somewhat useful though. I'm not discouraging counseling at all. It can be useful.

There are times I can't stop or control the unwanted behavior, the anger, the anxiety, or the deep sadness. The emotions I experience and exhibit frighten and overwhelm me as well as those around me. I act out in defense of these behaviors that are so difficult to endure. The patience of others is difficult but helps defuse these behaviors. When I lash out, I'm not myself. This has led to my being arrested on four separate occasions. Two of those arrests ended with me spending a day or two in a psychiatric facility where they didn't have an understanding of PTSD. The worst part was leaving the safety of my home and being thrust into an extremely hostile environment. The officers had no compassion. Even though I asked for medical help, especially after being without my medications for a day, I never received medical attention.

I have been told to "get over it." Unfortunately, I can't just "get over it." It saddens me to think that friends, and even relatives, could be so insensitive by such a statement; it has an inference that I like the condition I'm in, that I want to hold on to the pain. I had thought that after some time had passed that the memories would fade and life would get easier. However, because of the physiological changes associated with PTSD, the memories remain. My brain won't let me forget due to the chemical changes that occur from PTSD. Getting past the trauma of PTSD doesn't mean we will forget.

We've all seen the headlines implying that people with PTSD are dangerous. We must not resort to thinking, due to fear, that a person with PTSD equals a ticking time bomb. The stigma surrounding PTSD is so negative. It arouses concerns and provokes whispers and worried glances. People don't understand it at all. They assume I'm a potential powder keg just waiting for a spark to set me off into a rage, and that's just not true, about me or any person with PTSD. I have never physically assaulted anyone out of anger or rage. I'm suffering with it and people are afraid to ask me about it. However, I have been asked, "Do I need to worry?" My reply: "I have PTSD. I'm okay, and I'm not going to freak out on you."

All I want is a simple life, where I can relax and avoid having to talk about the cause, and enough time and solitude to recover from the horrors I have experienced. I need people to have patience enough to wait for me to reemerge. I am on a journey to find my way back to what once was a familiar place in my life. This journey has allowed me to find that I am a more capable person than I had ever imagined. There is so much more I now know about myself and about the world that others will never know or be able to understand.

It's extremely difficult to live with PTSD. It's a day-to-day struggle in which I no longer deny I have a problem. I know I have a condition that is not visible to others. I might look fine on the surface, but underneath I'm scrambling, trying to do the best

I can. The source of the problem lies deep within me. Sometimes it can become frustrating. Everything will be going along great and then it will change and I don't know why. I'm not sure if it is possible for me to overcome the trauma of PTSD. It may take years before I realize the depth of my injury. There are things that happen to you from which there is no recovery.

This was not the direction I would have chosen for my life.

It's not easy to accept a new way of living.

There's no going back.

———

Days seemed endless—
The nights even longer.
Three a.m. was two hours ago.
It wasn't fun when I crashed and burned.
I gave myself to strangers
In a job I loved to do;
Misplaced myself along the way.
My scars can't be seen.
I hold them on the inside
And fear the life I once knew,
When I tried to assimilate,
All I got were stares.
People don't see a wounded soul,
They just see someone to fear.
But I've seen too many fall,
So now I live within myself.
I was strong and brave.
And Hero was my name.

—James Meuer, 2012

———

CHAPTER 5

Children are born toward innocence. When they pretend, they know it is only pretending. They are filled with love and joy and are free to enjoy themselves.

How many adults are inspired by a child? Made to feel young and energetic? Or made to forget the stresses of life? Just watch a child play and you'll understand. He takes delight in life and savors every blessing. A child is honest and speaks what he thinks. And most of all, he believes what he is told and trusts implicitly. I have a hard time comprehending why children, why babies, die. It's a concept I can't wrap my head around.

I worked in one of the worst zones in our coverage areas. It was a low-income area filled with methamphetamine labs and members of a white supremacist group. There were nice homes intermingled with those in disrepair. Some of the poorer houses had chain-link fences around them and junk cars on the lawn. There were homes camouflaged in overgrown parcels of land. Entering some of these homes was frightening in itself. It seemed all but the nicest homes had just a few bare bulb lamps and a big dog growling at us from somewhere in the house.

It was a dark area with few working streetlights. The roads were two lanes, without curbs and unkempt which made driving them treacherous. At night, hidden potholes or sudden dips in the road were enough to throw the ambulance around or send us airborne if we weren't careful. There was also the occasional cow or horse running down the road. During the winter months a blanket of Tule fog would roll in, making it impossible to use the emergency lights (they would just reflect back at us) or to drive with any useful speed. The area included off-base housing for the local air force base.

It was there that I found the boy in the suitcase.

The shift had been slow and uneventful. When I say "uneventful" I mean the calls were for minor complaints and not of an urgent nature. It was a beautiful day. The sky was clear blue with few clouds. The temperature was comfortable, not too hot, and a jacket wasn't needed. I don't remember there being much of a breeze, which was unusual for that time of year.

The partner I had that day was new to the company. She and I had already worked a few shifts together and were starting to get a good rapport going. Sitting in the station that day we were in good moods. The phone rang and changed all that.

The dispatcher gave us a Code-3, a call for a sick child at the off-base housing. Code-3, at that time, meant using the siren and emergency lights. It also means driving fast yet safely. It gets the adrenaline pumping. Anytime a call came in for a sick child, it usually meant the child had a cold or high fever. In that area, an ambulance was some people's only ride to the hospital. I wasn't thinking it would be anything else. I definitely wasn't expecting to enter such a bizarre scene.

Whenever I was going Code-3, I usually lit a cigarette for the drive. This drive was no different. We arrived on scene to find that the fire department wasn't there yet. They usually arrived first. I found out later there was some confusion as to which fire district the call belonged. Nonetheless, I jumped out of the ambulance, tossing my cigarette down as I came around the back of the ambulance to get the gurney. My partner was grabbing the bags that contained various emergency supplies we might need. She heaved the bags onto the gurney, and we rushed to the house.

The front door opened as we approached. A young girl of maybe thirteen or fourteen greeted us. There were no other people in the house. The first thing I noticed was three or four suitcases by the front door. The house was completely empty of any furniture or personal items. I always took stock of the scene to get a feel for what might be happening. It was what we were taught, and it was very helpful on most calls. It appeared the occupants were moving out. I didn't think anything of it since it was base housing, and military personnel are often being deployed elsewhere. I figured the young girl was the sister or the babysitter of the child we were there to see. She directed us to a back bedroom. The only thing in the room was a crib and a suitcase.

"Where's the child you called about?" I asked politely, assuming she was the one who had called since she was the only person here.

"He's in the suitcase." She said it so calmly it sent a chill through me.

At first, for just a second, I thought she was kidding, but as I did a quick look around the room I realized she was serious. Then my partner and I both lunged for the suitcase. We laid it down and each popped a latch.

"Why is he in the suitcase?" My voice echoed through the empty house. Anyone who has lived in a base house knows how hollow they sound when they are empty.

The boy was unresponsive and barely breathing. His skin was pale and his eyes were half-open. I didn't see any obvious bleeding. He appeared to be about eighteen months old. I looked at the girl for answers, and all she did was shrug.

I was fuming inside as we treated the boy. My partner was attaching the heart monitor and setting up an IV while I was intubating. When I positioned his head to do this, I noticed a soft spot on his skull. I looked down his tiny throat using a laryngoscope, an instrument that allows me to find the vocal chords, so I could pass the endotracheal tube through them to assist his breathing. Once that was completed, a bag about the size of a small football was attached to the tube. Squeezing the bag forced air into his lungs to add more oxygen to his blood. I checked his little body for trauma, but other than the soft area of the skull, there wasn't any. There was not another mark on him. All I found was that one pupil was larger than the other, which can indicate trauma to the brain. I immediately thought the boy had been abused.

I told my partner to radio our dispatch to have a sheriff's officer meet us at the hospital. We weren't going to wait on-scene for them to arrive since I wasn't sure how long it would take them to arrive. It was more important to get the boy to a hospital.

The girl who had led us to the boy remained silent as I asked her questions:

"What happened to him?"

"Did he fall?"

"When did this happen?"

"Where are his parents?"

"Who put him in the suitcase?"

I paused slightly between each question. She just walked out of the room as we continued treating the boy. Due to the protocol in place for treating patients with trauma, we had to immobilize the boy's neck and back. For a child this small we would roll a towel and gently place it around the neck, being careful not to accidentally pull out the breathing tube. A rigid device called a KED, initially used in NASCAR to extricate drivers after a crash, was wrapped around his entire body. It was the simplest way to immobilize him and allow for him to be carried more easily while protecting him from further injury.

My partner was lifting the boy onto the gurney when the fire department arrived. So many thoughts were racing through my head. Who would stuff a severely injured baby in a suitcase? Did the girl do this and thought she could hide the boy? And where were his parents? I was so angry that the boy's parents weren't anywhere to be found that I wasn't listening to the fire department captain try to explain why they were delayed.

My partner cut him off. "Excuse me, but we've got to get going; the boy's got a bad head injury." she said politely. I had never heard her be rude with anybody or raise her voice. "My partner wants to start a line before we take off," she added.

She handed me the end of the IV tubing to connect to the catheter I had inserted into a tiny vein in his arm. He didn't flinch or make any sound. *That's not good,* I thought.

Then we headed to the ambulance. The fire crew grabbed our bags as my partner and I maneuvered the gurney out of the house. One of the firefighters rode with me in the back to help ventilate the boy and leave me free to handle other treatments that might arise. I reevaluated the boy. The soft spot was about three fingers in diameter and slightly to the left side on the back of his head. It was more than just a soft spot. It was a depressed skull fracture that was now starting to swell. His blood pressure was rising, and since the brain is enclosed in a confined space, it causes the brain to swell and squish out of the fracture site. His prognosis was getting worse. I knew the boy was going to die, but I kept working. At least this time I would have tried everything I could, and maybe I wouldn't feel guilty. As long as I tried what I could in my arsenal of tools to prevent death, I told myself I wouldn't feel guilty. It didn't work. I felt guilt for each dead baby I held, and he was no exception. I gave each one a piece of me. And I became more damaged.

I never found out what happened to "the boy in the suitcase," and I wanted it that way. If I never knew, then to me he was still alive, which made it easier for me to accept. It was a protective mechanism I developed. I never knew if there was an investigation; the sheriff's officer never spoke with me. In reality, the boy had died, and there was probably never an investigation.

Chapter 6

Not until we are lost do we begin to find ourselves.
—Henry David Thoreau

No one tells you the cost of being a paramedic. The job will harden you, making you cold to most emotions. I don't mean you'll never feel anything ever again, but if you want to survive the job, you have to learn to shut off some emotions, become clinical, stay objective, and do the job to the best of your abilities while trying to leave all the hurt, pain, and emotions behind. We can't expose our families to it. It will destroy relationships. If it's stored up and not dealt with, it will fester and slowly kill you.

In some cases it kills quicker. My frustration in not being able to communicate what was happening to me came out as anger. Anger is a basic survival instinct. For many people with PTSD, anger is a natural response and can make it harder to recover. Though that anger might be directed outward, too often it's focused inward. I couldn't tell anyone I crashed and burned because then I would become vulnerable. The chink in my armor would become visible and my weakness known.

In my struggle to comprehend what was happening to me, I started numbing myself with alcohol. The most prominent behavior I was exhibiting was anger, and alcohol gave me a break, even if for just a short time, from that anger. It also quieted the ghosts in my head that haunted me at night. I'm sure my wife had noticed a difference in my attitude, and maybe that's why she didn't want to listen anymore. She didn't understand, anyway. There was no way she could. My wife and I were constantly at odds with each other. I didn't know why I would fly into a rage over the simplest of things. While I never physically hurt anyone, there were a lot of walls that (literally) took my abuse. I didn't see the emotional strain I placed on my family. However, they saw me spiraling out of control and were as helpless as I was to stop it. Once the effects of the alcohol wore off the anger would return, but worse. It was as if all the anger I suppressed while drinking was stored up, just waiting for the time when I wasn't under the influence. The ghosts would also return, only louder.

One night while sitting home alone, I held a bottle of Jack Daniels in my left hand and a .357 revolver in my right. I just wanted not to hurt, and dying would be a quick answer. I thought if I had to hold one more dead baby, I would implode. The gun felt heavy in my hand while I was asking God to stop my pain so I wouldn't have to pull the trigger. I sat for a few hours drinking, spinning the cylinder, and loading and unloading a bullet. Deep inside I knew it was out of the question. I would never leave my daughter or my family. Besides, I truly believe suicide is a sin, and it's not a solution. It leaves others behind with questions and to pick up the pieces. I knew my dad and mom would have taken it the hardest. My daughter was still a baby and my wife had filed for divorce. She didn't care anymore. Even though I was raised in a strong Christian family, my faith had wavered, but I had a sense that God had a purpose in my being alive, and that was all that kept me going. I wanted to see why he wanted me so badly and in turn find out the purpose. With the effects of the alcohol and the heavy tears, I couldn't see well enough to put the bullet back in the cylinder. I was both laughing at myself trying to load the gun and crying as I set the gun on the coffee table, silently saying, "Thank you, God."

I honestly didn't have a death wish then or now. I did, however, put myself in more dangerous situations at work with the thought that if something did happen to me, then I really wasn't killing myself.

Life felt like such drudgery. To liven it up I frequently went out to bars with friends from work. I was losing any desires to do things that I usually enjoyed or made me happy. I didn't feel alive unless I was at work surrounded by the only people who could possibly understand the stress of the job. There is a camaraderie amongst first responders that is rarely found in any other profession. Living with people for twenty-four hours at a time, you eventually get to know them well. I'd share certain things with my partner I never would share with anyone else. Even though we were a tight-knit bunch, they weren't a healthy support group. I feared letting them know I was in trouble. They wouldn't understand. After all, burning out was a sign of weakness, and I didn't and still don't consider myself weak. Nor did I think I was burning out. Letting them see me cry was totally out of the question. I felt it would be a death sentence as a paramedic if they saw me cry. As a first responder, if you need to go to counseling, then you're considered weak. And we are not allowed to be weak in EMS. As first responders, we're not supposed to feel this way. In truth, we do.

Craving the one thing that made me feel alive, I worked massive amounts of overtime. Working forty-eight—to seventy-two-hour shifts kept me away from the tensions at home and allowed me to feel alive for a short time.

When I wasn't at work I didn't want to be around people. I just wanted to be by myself. After my divorce I bought a motorcycle, a Suzuki Katana 600. Riding was solitude. I craved the adrenaline rush riding a motorcycle gave me. Around this same time I also wasn't on the best of speaking terms with my family. They were upset with my divorce and my in-your-face attitude I had developed. My anger and drinking had caused a rift in my family dynamic. I avoided talking to or calling anyone, not just my family. In my self-isolation, I would listen to music. It was great for relaxation and helped me escape the various stressors I was experiencing. I could be having the worst day in the world, but if I listened to the right song at the right time, it just made my day a little better. Music gave a voice to my feelings. The louder the volume, the easier it was to drown out my emotions. I needed to not feel them. I wanted not to feel.

I became one person at work and another at home. We all try to keep our work out of our home life and vice versa, but keeping the two separate is near impossible when you're hurting, and I was hurting. At work I could block out the chaos encountered on a scene and take charge. I kept my emotions in check, got the job done, and moved on to the next without talking about the call. At home it was a different story. I didn't know how to turn my emotions back on, which made me withdrawn. The garbage from the previous day's work followed me through the door. In the beginning, I would come home and share with my wife what my shift was like. Toward the end of that marriage I realized she didn't care and couldn't provide healthy feedback anyway. I started keeping all the pain inside. At home my thoughts were constantly racing, but I never stopped to focus on one. A day at home was spent without rest going from one menial task to the next: laundry, dishes, yard work, etc. All I really wanted to do was sit on the couch and watch television, but that didn't always happen. When I tried to relax I would think through the previous day's shift, run through the calls again, and criticize my actions and decisions.

So many times I wanted to give up. Anyone can give up; it's the easy way. Anyone who knew what I was going through would understand if I fell to pieces, but no one knew. I've never taken the easy route; I kept looking for the road to save myself.

Fleeting glances, lack of hope,
Requital for being a hero.
Afraid to let my secrets out
But too scared to face my fears.
Try to fight the darkness,
Too weak to make the stand,
The walls I built to keep me safe
Are only made of glass.
I don't want you to see me—
Then you'll know who I am.
After I started collecting ghosts,
All I had left were the stories
Giving birth to the fear of fear.
I may be silent but my brain never is,
Nor is it subtle.
I've felt overwhelmed,
Went beyond what I could handle
And found how strong I was
After I had been broken.

—James Meuer, 2012

CHAPTER 7

I know who I am and what I've been through, what I can handle, and how strong I am. However, I am nothing special; there will be no monuments dedicated to me, and my name will soon be forgotten. There are many more that have done the same as I have. Others have experienced more in their lives, others less. Some have come away unscathed while others suffer in silence. When you get on the ambulance, you don't know what it is God will be calling you to do. EMS is certainly a calling. It stays with you even after you've left the job.

I lasted twenty-six years in EMS, way beyond the average career expectancy of five years for an EMT. The EMS profession is somewhat unique in comparison to others. First responders are prepared to sacrifice their own lives to save the lives of others. I am still willing to do it, but my mind and body don't allow me. Being a paramedic was often rewarding, but at times it was unnerving. It's a profession that shows no mercy for the preciousness of life or those that do the job. A first responder will, without hesitation, enter into some of the most inhospitable places and situations that most people will never know exist. The line-of-duty death rate of paramedics is comparable to firefighters and police officers. Why did I put myself in a job where I might never again lay eyes on my loved ones? I gave up even trying to surmise an answer. At times I do think about the people I met and maybe even saved. I look back on the years of my life I gave being a paramedic and hope I made a difference. Many times I look back through eyes blurred by tears. I can't block out the past forever, but I can't afford to remember.

The job started to determine the amount of hours I worked, the mental toll it took, and also the personality I developed. My personality certainly became a reflection of the job. All the things I complained about in the profession—odd hours, sleep deprivation, financial strain, and high stress—were major contributors to my marital problems.

My first marriage ended after only four years. Divorce is common among many professions, EMS being one of them. I became married to the job, and the station I worked out of became "my house." My wife at that time didn't like my job or the odd hours I worked. I would come home in the morning tired and emotionally drained after a long shift and just want to fall into bed. At other times when I came home I needed to talk and a shoulder to lean on. In the beginning she was there for me, but by the end of the marriage she didn't want to listen. I can't share my work with those I love. I can't tell them what I've seen lying in an alley or in a seedy hotel room. I can't describe the hair matted with blood, or external organs displayed in the street, or the paraplegic with wounds filled with maggots. At the time I thought my wife turned her back to me. In reality I had turned my back on the marriage, although not intentionally. I hadn't seen my behavior—the anger, the drinking, the being emotionally withdrawn—as contributing factors.

I was remarried within a year of the end of my first marriage. This time I thought it would be different, but I was never more wrong. It was more of the same arguments, angry days, and sleepless nights. We had two children, a girl and a boy, and also had one son die at birth. I continued to give myself to the job and to lose pieces of myself along the way. My attitude was getting worse; I withdrew more into myself, stopped talking about work completely, and also kept drinking. My doctor prescribed one antidepressant after another and told me to seek counseling. I tried going to counseling, but insurance would only cover a few visits, so it was sporadic. The antidepressants took too long to work to have any benefit and I was impatient. I wanted to sleep and the dreams to stop.

The job also took a toll on me physically. I was involved in two accidents while in the ambulance. In one I was the driver, the other I was in the back with a patient. There were patients who wanted to fight; one pulled a knife on me. I fractured one of the small bones in my wrist and tore a bicep tendon in separate incidents. After many years of poor lifting techniques, it seemed the larger the patient, the smaller the space they had to be extricated from; I was diagnosed with a ruptured disc in my lower back. I had back surgery six years after the diagnosis, a month after 9/11. Somewhere along the way I fractured a vertebra in my neck and one in my back. Needless to say the job broke me in many ways. With all the injuries and the surgery, I developed an addiction to painkillers. Vicodin became my best friend. It helped me sleep, it stopped the dreams, and I could tolerate life.

By this time I would have to say my life had deteriorated. I was hurting physically, mentally, and spiritually. I had built up a tolerance to the Vicodin to the point where I was taking thirty to forty pills at a time twice a day. If I was having a rough day and didn't have the pills, I would drink. The memories and dreams were loud and clear when I didn't self-medicate. It was a miserable existence. Still I continued because I just wanted the dreams and memories to stop.

One day my ten year old daughter couldn't wake me. That was the proverbial wake-up call and a strong incentive to stop the Vicodin. I tried a few different methods prior to this to stop my addiction, but I always eventually started taking the pills again. It was during a seven-day detox that my wife had taken our two children and moved out. She had been threatening divorce if I didn't stop taking the Vicodin, but I didn't take her seriously; after all, she had been threatening it for years. The marriage ended after fourteen years.

One night while I was sitting alone in the house I had an idea. Since I wasn't sleeping much anyway, I might as well stay awake. That bright idea ended in a six-month cocaine binge. I spent everything I had on drugs, trying to forget and not feel.

CHAPTER 8

I think it's very healthy to spend time alone. You need to know
how to be alone and not defined by another person.
—Oscar Wilde

The blood of the dead will wash out of the uniform, but you
can't wash the memories out of your brain. You see the faces as
if the person is standing right in front of you. Like a friend has
come to visit—an old friend who visits whenever he wants and
hangs around for a little, stirring things up in your head. Then
when all the things that have been locked away, long forgotten,
are awakened, that friend leaves. When you finally get things
quieted, another will come calling with the sole intention to whip
it all into a frenzy.

Most people can walk around their town or city and see the
shops, cars, and people all busily heading somewhere. I walk
around that same city, and all I see is a battlefield—a house where a
battle to save a life failed, or an intersection and time spent cutting
teenagers out of a wrecked car. It's a torturous existence.

Like so many of us with PTSD surrounded by what should
be the familiar, we often find ourselves feeling a sense of being
displaced. I understand what feeling displaced is like. Many times
I felt alienated in my own town, even among friends. It's a daily
struggle being in pain or feeling sick on the inside while you look
fine on the outside. I know what it's like to talk and have nobody
understand, to feel alone, and to fight to get back to my family.

It's like carrying around a glass jar filled with all the memories, dreams, faces, and fears. Every so often the lid gets loose and some stuff leaks out. You tighten the lid and carry this jar around, being careful not to break it, so you hold on to it tightly. You do whatever you can to keep that lid on because you know what happens when the lid gets loose. You definitely don't want the lid to come off completely because that's when hell breaks loose. You drink or do drugs to keep the lid tight. You protect that jar with everything you have, never letting your guard down. You can't help but be that way. It's not as if you can help it. You would love for it to not be that way, but you have to protect that jar.

I couldn't keep drinking or using drugs to prevent the jar from breaking or to silence the dreams and memories. But I couldn't live with them either. The methods I was using weren't working. Due to the drug use, my money was gone, and I wasn't allowed to see my children. I was still having anger issues; I couldn't get along with the people at work. Sleep hadn't visited me in years. The flashbacks were becoming more frightening. I worried I would have one in public, so I locked myself indoors at my parents' house three states away from my kids and away from the world. I was planning to never leave the house except when necessary and with enough notice to prepare.

This painful ending gave way to a new beginning.

Things didn't change quickly for me. But it was a start. The first thing I realized was that I couldn't carry on at the pace I was going. It was slowly killing me. I had to be the one to change what I was doing in order to make it easier to deal with PTSD. I had plenty of time to think. What I decided to do first was confront my grief.

Grief is not a sign of weakness. It is an emotional and physical response to a heavy feeling of sadness. The only cure for grief is to grieve. As first responders, we don't grieve. We let it all build up until there is such heaviness it's unbearable, and we become imprisoned within ourselves. I allowed myself to recall situations I was involved in and to cry for the dead. Cry as hard as you want, but just make sure when you're finished you never cry for the same reason again. This is much easier said than done.

No matter the circumstances, don't expect immediate results. I had to remember that it's all right not to know the answers, that they will come to me when I least expect it and that I don't own all the problems in the world. I had been so worried about what others might think of me if they knew I had PTSD that it paralyzed me. I was afraid to be me. It wasn't until a special woman came into my life that I came to understand that it's not what others think, it's what I think about myself that matters. What others think of me is not my concern. I own my PTSD. I was no longer going to run from it.

I was never going to leave where I was until I decided where I'd rather be, which was in California. I figured out what I wanted and went after it. It had been almost two years since I'd locked myself away at my parents' house. I don't like going out and especially hate driving, but I took a huge leap of faith. One day I packed everything I owned into my truck and drove two thousand miles from Texas to California for the love of a great woman and to get back to my kids. The drive was frightening for me. There were many times I wanted to turn around and head back to my already-established safe zone.

I didn't know it then, but God was laying groundwork for healing. I was seeking out friends from the past who were from a better time. In this process I found a friend I had attended Christian school with thirty-two years prior. When we first met I had no idea she would become so important to me. We struck up a conversation through a social media site and became attached immediately. When I thought I would never have another relationship, God sends Tracy to me. We spent months talking for hours; nothing was held back. Tracy supported me without fail. She said she knew my heart. Then she said she trusted me. That was all it took. Her support, despite my past, was amazing.

Taking a leap of faith for all the right reasons is one of the scariest things a person can do. I believe it was Eleanor Roosevelt who said, "Do one thing each day that scares you."

"The Bridge of Fear"

I stepped boldly, without hesitation, brazenly assuming heights of grandeur. My feet began strong, with purpose, yet strangely became weighted as my eyes enveloped severe vastness surrounding my every move. My vision narrowed, and my breath labored near cessation. The rise and fall of my chest became slavery. My hands tightened, restricting the life-flowing blood—a chameleon void of color.

Panic embraced me as I seek refuge. Once-familiar faces blur and bend until they disappear. I can only hear my heart as a deafening drum. My tears flow but restrained to silence as I am captive. The distance a lifetime away yet nearing to the end, I crave salvation. As my feet leave the bridge I am able to inhale for the first time. Reviving my oxygen-starved brain, my shoulders are released from their soldier's stance. My view widened and my soul wept. Shame overwhelmed me as I now got a glance of myself. I feel humbled and alone. How will I resolve to bridge this gap of fear?

—Tracy Castelli, 2003

CHAPTER 9

> The world ain't all sunshine and rainbows. It's a very mean and
> nasty place. And I don't care how tough you are; it will beat
> you to your knees and keep you there if you let it. You me or
> nobody is going to hit as hard as life. But it ain't about how hard
> you can hit, it's about how hard you can get hit and keep moving
> forward; how much you can take and keep moving forward.
> —"Rocky," *Rocky Balboa*

In life, we do things. Some we wish we had never done and some
we wish we could replay over and over. But that is what makes
us who we are in the end. And when you think things are falling
apart, maybe everything is really falling into place.

I am alone and sad. I cry all night and no one sees me since
I am alone. All the time, day or night, I pray for it to end. I am
clad in black even though there is no funeral, but all around me
people wear masks on their "happy" faces for a show. I long for
the time before PTSD.

The Greek word for "return home," *nostos*, is the root of our
word "nostalgia," along with *algos,* meaning "pain" or "sorrow."
The word nostalgia was first coined as a medical term in 1688 by
a Swiss medical student to describe the psychological condition
some soldiers exhibited. More commonly, nostalgia refers to an
interest in past eras and events, especially the "good old days." This
is a good description of the feelings that someone with PTSD
experiences.

It's not the future that I'm afraid of. It's repeating the past that makes me anxious. It's not what I have been through in my life that has defined who I am, it's how I got through it that has made me the person I am today. No matter how any times I break down, there is always a piece of me that says, "Get back up!" Out of my suffering has emerged a strong soul. The most massive characters are seared with scars. It is tempting to hide my emotional scars, but I should actually display them as a testament to how I have survived and how God has brought me through. I'm not perfect; I've made a lot of mistakes. But I really appreciate those people who stand by me especially after knowing who I really am.

- First, never sacrifice a good life for a good time—it's never worth it.
- Second, don't judge me. It's possible you couldn't handle half of what I've been through or dealt with. There's a reason I've done the things I've done, a reason I do the things I do, and a reason I am who I am. I'm not a hero; I don't deserve to be called a hero. I'm just an inauspicious man locked in a box. The box is my safe zone.
- Third, don't believe everything you think.

Everyday, somebody out there is being told to learn to live with this. Everyday, somebody out there is being denied disability. Everyday, somebody out there is not getting support from family and friends. Everyday, somebody out there thinks he or she is alone. Everyday, somebody out there is wondering if he or she can do this.

I have learned how to be content with whatever I have. I know how to live on almost nothing or with everything, with a full stomach or empty. Could I have learned these lessons without the trauma? Probably, but it might have taken longer.

Let me try to explain a medic or any first responder.

I hope you understand.

He (or she) is addicted to the job, although he loves his family. Inasmuch that death is horrible, there is nothing like a life-and-death fight to make him feel truly alive. The adrenaline rush is huge, and it can never be replaced. Being a paramedic means he is in a brotherhood where he is always understood; just ask any retired medic.

Being present for his family is harder. It would be easy for him to die for his family, but living for them, which is what they actually want, is harder for him. It is even harder for him if they don't need him to rescue them, since rescuing is his job, his gift, his joy, and his curse, which may lead him to question if he is needed at all. He may not see that his family chooses to stay with him.

A first responder has the ability to respond to an emergency with minimal time for consciously thinking about options. While this is a benefit for his job, it is not helpful in the slower-paced world. The adrenaline rush he gets from the job is absent in the real world. This can result in explosive emotions that can be difficult to control. Unfortunately, that can lead to exhibiting outbursts of explosive anger toward friends, family, or, unfortunately, strangers.

He is afraid to get attached to anyone because he doesn't want to be exposed; he doesn't want them to know who he is, and he cannot face that pain. He may make an exception for his children (because they cannot divorce him). I say "may make an exception" because there are some first responders who go into total isolation. This choice will be instinctual, and he will probably not be able to explain his actions.

He may not know how to feel about what he's seen or done. He can experience moments of intense guilt, shame, and self-hatred. Over the course of a shift, he may experience a moment of elation because he saved a life and then wonder why he couldn't save another. The bewilderment from these emotions can be confusing.

He may think he's the only one who has ever felt this way and may not want to reveal himself because he doesn't want to be thought of as weak. He may never learn there are others who understand. He wants to turn to family for support, but part of him doesn't want his family to understand because then they would have to share his dreadful experiences, and he doesn't want them exposed to those horrors. He doesn't want his family to become a casualty of his battle. Although they may be in the midst of the battle, his issues aren't about them.

What may be difficult to understand is that he needs his family to believe in the good in him, rather than something bad, when they have the possibility of doing either.

CHAPTER 10

There is no passion to be found in settling for a life
that is less than the one you are capable of living.
—Nelson Mandela

When I locked myself away in my parents' house, it was symbiotic.
I helped them with the upkeep of the house, yard work, and any
medical issues that arose, and I had my safe zone. I had to do what
was best for me, not what was best for everyone else. At the time,
it was best for me to distance myself from the world. It gave me
time to decompress, time to think, and time to heal; time heals
almost everything. I could accept the conditions of PTSD as they
existed or take the responsibility for changing them. It mattered
what I was going to do, not what I had done. I had to take time
to recognize and appreciate the present. I had lost sight of all the
beauty that surrounded me; the greatest part of life is made up of
the little things. I'm the only one in charge of my happiness.

This is my battle, and this is how it all changed. You may fix
it your way or choose to sit and wait it out—trust me, that doesn't
work—but this is how it got better for me.

I tried hiding, running, drinking it away, and doing enough
drugs to kill the proverbial horse yet nothing made it better until
I gave it to God, gave in to God and his plan for me. Even if you
don't believe in God, he just might be there.

A few years earlier I had hit the lowest point in my life.
Because of my attitude and anger I felt as if my family didn't want

me around. I was broke, I was having a hard time keeping a job and getting along with coworkers, and Vicodin was tempting me again. I ran away. Or at least I tried. I went to Riyadh, Saudi Arabia, for a one-year contract as a medic at a National Guard hospital. There I wouldn't be allowed a Bible, and since drugs and alcohol are also banned I wouldn't have that temptation. Even though I had been brought up in a Christian household and had attended private Christian school, some years prior I swore I would never set foot in a church again; I had cussed God out for putting me in the mess I was in, for giving up on me, and for just not caring. When I returned from Riyadh, I was angrier and more withdrawn than before I left the states. I remained in this bitter, angry state for four years until I locked myself away.

I had lost everything and ended back in my parents' house. This complete loss reminded me of my deepest values, of what's really important, and that there's more to life than bigger houses, expensive vacations, and a closet full of clothes. Without this great loss I wouldn't have been so willing to step back into God's hands. He allowed me to hit the lowest point in my life and waited for me to reach out to him. If God hadn't done it this way, I would have thought I had done it on my own. I can do nothing apart from him.

One day I drove my mom to the church I had attended when I first moved to Texas eight years prior. While I waited in the parking lot, she came out to the car to tell me a friend I knew from when I attended earlier wanted me to come in. I went in apprehensively, almost expecting a lightening bolt to strike me. I hadn't been in a church for more than five years. I was accepted back as if I hadn't been gone at all. That was the beginning of renewing my faith and of my spiritual healing. This was when things started to change for the better.

It was time to make peace with God and in turn make peace with my past with hopes it wouldn't screw up the present. It took me a while to understand that my past doesn't equal my future. I don't want to be judged by my past, just as I'm sure others don't want to be judged by theirs. One mistake doesn't have to control your life. Don't compare your life to others' and don't judge them. You have no idea what their journey is all about, just as they don't know yours. The past needs to be left in the past.

I learned right away that God is very forgiving. He is a God of second chances. And I needed a second chance. Or a third . . . I also needed to forgive. It was time to make decisions and not excuses, time to face my issues and fix what I could.

I had tried to make order in my world to make it predictable and feel safe. This is a totally impractical goal. Instead of trying for a problem-free life, I chose to lean on God and stop trying to do things my way. A lot of our hurts come from relationships so it makes sense that healing can also come from them. I received healing through having a relationship with God. I also wanted to heal my relationships with my children. I'm sure I look different and may not make sense to those hearing me say these things, especially if they knew me years ago.

I had been angrily lashing out at everything and everybody. I wanted to be in control, just like I tried to control everything else in my life. I was a broken mess, just scattered pieces of who I was. I tried so hard. I thought I could do it on my own, but I had lost so much along the way. When I see what has been accomplished, I know I'm finally God's. I found everything I thought I'd lost before. He called my name; I came to him in pieces and he made me whole. I had come undone, but he makes sense of who I am. Giving your life over to God's control doesn't mean being complacent. It means understanding that he has a plan and we're not the one in control.

I allowed God to rescue me—or I should say I gave in to him. God had seen me cry myself to sleep, had seen my faithfulness, and he wanted me to know that the storm is almost over. The storms of life may be raging all around you, but God is always there to bring you through. In the midst of the storm, reach out to God, who calms the tempestuous sea and gives you peace. It was God who rescued me. He came to be my friend and companion. It is that story that makes me know how important he is to those of us who suffer from something where others can't see the physical scars.

I have never served in the military but can relate to those overwhelming feelings that can overtake and consume. I have spent more years than I should have where I shouldn't have been. So basically as a result of choices on my part, choices I would make again because I loved the job, these symptoms visit me. It seems I'm always extricating myself from a place that takes me back to those memories and keeps me from living and enjoying life to its fullest, a life as God intended. However, I seem to end up in situations that take me back. The time I stay is shorter, and over time the effects have become not as profound. I no longer sit in the dark in fear. I do go out, but it is not totally without feeling anxious, jittery, or irritated and always thinking I'm in danger. I sometimes get a sense of panic that something bad is about to happen.

Driving down the roads in one of the towns I used to work, I found myself noticing every piece of debris, avoiding every pothole, feeling upset by things that reminded me of what happened, having vivid memories and flashbacks of events that make me feel like it's happening all over again. When I had stress brought on by flashbacks, I dealt with them by drinking them away. I considered it recreational drinking, but really I was self-medicating. When alcohol stopped working, I moved on to abusing drugs. At first I abused prescription medications and then street drugs. I was constantly drinking or using drugs to numb my feelings. Nothing totally stopped what was going on in my head. Some can turn it off like a light, but I can't; for me, the light never goes out.

With the Lord's guidance I was able to reach the point where it is now God I rely on instead of drugs and alcohol. Sometimes things still go wrong, and my burdens get hard to bear, and it may seem that no one cares, but I know God has me covered. Whenever you don't understand what's happening in your life, just close your eyes, take a deep breath and say, "God, I know it is your plan, so just help me through it." When you let God take full control of your life, his plan will be full-speed ahead. Just hang on for the ride because he will take you to places you never could have imagined you would go. Always keep the faith. He is waiting for you to ask so he can show you the way.

When all seems lost and you feel there is no hope left, remember that this time will pass, and you will look back and see how it has made you stronger. I am not alone; I am not facing the struggles and challenges of life by myself—God is with me.

"'For I know the plans I have for you,' declares the Lord, "plans for welfare and not for evil, to give you a future and a hope'" (Jeremiah 29:11, English Standard Version). Whenever you feel lost or off course, look to and remember this, for God's plans are good.

★

The shooting in Sandy Hook, Connecticut, on December 14, 2012, has opened a wound I had never felt until now. I felt such pain and intense sadness not only for the people who died but for the first responders who had to enter that scene. It had to be utter chaos. They, the medics, have no clue and probably aren't thinking of the emotional stress their minds will put them through. They won't comprehend why they are in a slump. Surely they will talk to their wives, husbands, family, or friends, limiting how much information they share. They will ultimately blame their slump on the responding to the call and the sight they endured, but there will always be a feeling, a twinge, something nagging at them that they can't shake. It will be quiet at times and not so subtle at other times. Their brain won't allow them to forget. And I will feel it for them and pray.

CHAPTER 11

Here are just a few symptoms of PTSD:

- feeling emotionally cut off from others
- feeling numb or losing interest in things you used to care about
- becoming depressed
- having difficulty sleeping
- having trouble keeping your mind on one thing
- having a hard time relating to and getting along with your spouse, family, or friends
- frequently avoiding places or things that remind you of what happened

The reason I bring these up again is to remind you it's not just the symptoms of PTSD but also how you may react to them that can disrupt your life. Heavy drinking and trauma often go hand in hand. People with drinking problems are more likely than others to experience a trauma. And people with PTSD who drink too much can't see when their PTSD symptoms, like sleep problems, anger, and relationship problems, worsen. If trauma, PTSD, and heavy drinking are part of your life, you can take steps to try to overcome them.

Some people may feel they need treatment but aren't quite ready to take the plunge. They are unwilling, afraid, or too fearful. You have to ask yourself, "How long do I want to suffer?"

"Will it do any good?," and "Does it help?" I was skeptical of those with a PhD and psychologists saying they could help me with my PTSD—after all, how do they know what will work? They had never been through it.

For many first responders, memories of their experiences can still be upsetting long after they have left the job. If you are an older first responder, you may have served many years ago, but your job experience can still affect your life today.

Many older first responders find they have PTSD symptoms even twenty or more years after their experience. There are a number of reasons symptoms of PTSD may increase with age. Having retired from work may make your symptoms feel worse because you have more time to think and fewer things to distract you from your memories. Having medical problems and feeling like you are not as strong as you used to be also can increase symptoms. You may find that bad news on the television and scenes from current news shows bring back bad memories.

If you have tried to cope with stress by using alcohol or other substances and you stop drinking without first finding another, healthier way of coping, it can make PTSD symptoms seem worse. PTSD symptoms can occur soon after a traumatic experience, but this is not always the case.

Some first responders begin to have PTSD symptoms soon after they had a bad call. These symptoms may last until older age. Other medics don't have PTSD symptoms until later in life. For some, PTSD symptoms can be extreme right after the experience, may decrease over the years, and then worsen again later in life.

Many older first responders have functioned well since their experience. Then later in life they begin to think more or become more emotional about their job experience. As you age, it is normal to look back over your life and try to make sense of your experiences. Having symptoms later in life is not upsetting for all first responders. While some find that remembering their experience is upsetting, many find that it helps them to make meaning of their job.

If you know someone with PTSD, never ask him or her what caused it unless you want a storm to hit. There is no straight response, Try to understand the blackness, hopelessness, and loneliness the person is going through. Be there for this person when he or she is ready to share. It may be hard to be his or her friend, but it will be the kindest and noblest thing you can do to help.

No one has it all figured out, especially the people who are acting like they do and judging you because of it. Pretending to be something you aren't because you're trying to please a bunch of judgmental hypocrites is not the way to be happy. Living the life God gave you according to his plan is the way. It really is that simple.

It is a time when grieving, pain, and angst, loneliness, and fear surface. This is the time when you need to realize that the only thing you can do is let them know you love them, care for them, and you will be there for them no matter what. Sometimes just sitting close can mean everything. Always remember that in some way or another you're somebody's angel, even if you (or they) don't know it. They love you and think of you even if you don't hear it everyday. Trust that there is love all around you even if you can't feel it. You're not alone.

Find one person who wants to help, one you feel you can trust. Tell that person you will let him or her in. To make sure he or she really wants in, say you are going to share some heavy, intense stuff. Share one story, dream, or flashback, and don't hold back, and you'll know if he or she really wants to (or can) help. The person will either cut you off, stop you, and run away or will hold you and make some physical contact with you. You'll know if he or she is the one. The first to help you up are the ones who know what it feels like to fall.

CHAPTER 12

I had been through drug treatment programs that use the 12-steps. The first two steps are admitting you are powerless to control the situation and admitting there is a higher power greater than yourself who can restore you. True restoration comes only from Christ. Counselors and medications can control the symptoms, but only through Christ you can find rest and comfort. He understands your pain.

The third step is to make a decision to turn your will and your life over to the care of God *as we understand him.*

I was a mess before I gave my life back to Jesus. I was addicted to drugs, alcohol, and cigarettes for years. I hated getting out of bed in the morning. My self-esteem was so low that I didn't feel like going out anymore. I just wanted to hide away from the world, so I did. I was reclusive, afraid to talk to people, even my own friends. I became a shell of myself. I felt dead on the inside. I hit rock bottom. This is what PTSD had brought me.

In desperation I cried out to Jesus. I begged him to help me. I cried and apologized for wasting my life, for hurting my family, and for completely destroying myself. I couldn't take this life anymore, but I knew suicide wasn't an option. When I asked the Lord Jesus to direct my life, and when I asked him for forgiveness, I surrendered myself completely to him. And in the midst of my torment he reached down and lifted me from the wreckage. He opened my heart up to receive his Spirit, and I felt his love fill and flow through me. I felt such a sense of pure joy that it literally took my breath away. I will never forget it. It was an absolutely life-changing moment. I was delivered from years of addictions; no drug can compare to the feeling the Lord can give. That type of peace is what we all long for and try to fill with materialistic items, but that kind of feeling can only comes from one source.

I had reached the end of my rope, and I was losing my grip. I opened my dusty Bible, and as I read I could not stop the flow of tears. It became clear that the life I had been living was aimless and what I had accepted as normal didn't have to be. I fell on my knees too weak to stand.

It was in that moment that I met God for the second time in my life. I felt a wave of serenity wash over me. I could sense joy and peace surround me. I saw the Lord standing with open arms. I called to him, "Lord, I am filthy, tired, and I don't want you to see me like this. I can't come to you where you can see my face and the shame I'm hiding."

I heard his voice, peaceful and soothing yet able to move mountains. "Don't be afraid. I've been waiting for you. Come to me. I know you are thirsty and I have water. I know you are hungry and I have plenty for you to eat."

I said, "Lord, you don't know me and I don't deserve a place at your table."

The Lord replied, "I do know you, and you can come home."

I had been chained by self-pity; the chains were heavy, and each time I tried to free myself, they tightened. Each time I tried to free myself I became more tangled in my past, my worthlessness, my addictions, the harm I had caused, the hearts I had broken, and the lives I had shattered. I kept putting on more chains; I could hear voices calling to me from behind, "You can't leave us; you belong with us."

I heard the Lord say again, "Come home, Son; it's time for you to come home."

I replied, "But Lord, I am worthless. I have wasted my talents and broken your commandments. Lord, I have done things from which I cannot return. I have lived in the darkness so long I can no longer see the light. I have wallowed in sin and have danced with the devil."

A cold chill went through me. I felt alone and desolate, and I felt the chains pulling me back while the voices echoed, "You belong with us."

At that moment a bright light, brighter than anything I had ever seen appeared. I was blinded. I wanted to cover my face but its warmth and peace that dwelled within it was alluring. Then came a loud voice, "I do not care what you have done, I do not care what you have become, just come home because I love you."

I reached down toward the locks on the chains that had held me for so long. The chains had become rusted and they crumbled in my hands. The weight of the world fell from my shoulders. The past didn't matter anymore, and I realized I was free and no longer bound.

I turned and ran toward the Lord; I sprinted as fast as my legs would move me. I heard the deafening screams behind me urging me to turn around and come back, begging me to give them another chance, trying to fill my mind with the thoughts I was not worthy of the Lord. I saw him just a short distance away. I ran into his arms, speechless and with tears flowing down my cheeks.

He simply said, "Welcome home, Son, welcome home. I have prepared a feast for you."

He held his hands up toward the heavens, and I saw blood flowing from them. I fell to my knees and looked down to see blood flowing from his feet.

He stated, "This is my child, and his name is forever written in the Book of Life. His sins have been paid for by the blood that flows from my body, and he is now forever sealed as a son in my Father's house. He now has the power over you, Satan, over the principalities of darkness, and from this day forward there is no condemnation for him; his sins are forgiven and his slate is washed cleaned by my blood."

I saw a bloodstained cross, and it kept the past and the demons at bay, held their death while giving me life. He held up his hands and said, "Father, your son has come back home; he was lost but has been found again; he is scarred and battered, but he is home and now he is whole."

God's love affects every aspect of my life. It affects how I think, what I feel, what I choose, how I spend my money; it affects my attitude toward people, toward the world, and toward myself. I had a life-changing encounter with God that convinced me beyond all doubt that God is real, that Jesus is his Son, that Jesus was crucified for sinners and was raised from the dead, and that he is the Savior of the world. I believe in the eternal existence of the soul and the eternal judgment of all persons. I believe all are sinners and God has made provision for the salvation of all men through faith in the redemptive death of his Son. Because of this I strive to always maintain a good conscience before God and men, and to promote the Gospel by whatever means I find.

This has brought me great peace and contentment, been a source of strength through difficulties, and has been an inspiration to try to improve. It's made me appreciative of life and all it has to offer, has reminded me that the good outweighs the bad, and has taught me that I really do have control, although God has the ultimate control, over my life and that it all lies in my choices and in how I react to things. It can be overwhelming when difficult challenges are put into our lives. I have found it best to give it to him because he is greater than all things combined. I used to carry the load myself, and when I gave it all to him, my load not only became lighter, I could see clearer.

At times it can be difficult to remain positive when negativity surrounds you, but you have full control over your attitude. A body of water the size of the entire ocean can't sink a ship unless it gets inside the ship. Similarly, all the negativity in the world can't bring you down unless you allow it to get inside your head. People who are able to remain positive in negative situations are the ones who prosper in the long run. So defend yourself against the "negative way" and make room for a positive day. This world is full of beautiful people who know you have worth. Just because there is someone who still doesn't have the wisdom to appreciate you doesn't mean you lack anything. It just means the person is blocked with a limited capacity to know the real you. Don't let his or her foolishness keep you down. Let the person take his or her own time getting out of a constricted view. With God's will and prayer, all things are possible.

My life has taken an amazing turn. I try to live the life the Lord wants me to lead, and the rewards are greater than any I could have imagined. Jesus has given my life a purpose and meaning, and I no longer take it for granted. I feel happy to be alive. My worldview has definitely been affected because now, where I once felt fear, I feel compassion. Many other people are just like I used to be, lost and lonely, and just wanting to be loved and accepted. I'm reaching out to them to help them the same way God helped me. I only hope more people will know the joy I have come to know.

Not everybody is going to have that person in their life that wholly supports them, or parents like mine who taught me about God and took me to church. Each of us has our own flaws. We are all broken vessels. But it is the uniqueness of our flaws that make our lives together so interesting and rewarding. People come from different places, but what I've discovered is God provided me peace, and a new safe zone. I'm not telling you how to do it; I'm telling you how I did it. I tried drugs, I tried alcohol, but nothing worked until I gave in to God. I may be damaged, but I'm not useless. I'm not alone anymore. God has filled the empty spaces, piecing me back together like a beautiful mosaic.

But I am still a work in progress. I didn't just wake up one morning and everything was perfect. My days are peaceful and the anger I had is but a memory. I still avoid going out, but I can go outside more easily now. The flashbacks and dreams are fewer, and the fear and anxiety have let up. I'm not entirely free from the affects of PTSD. The truth is I may never be free from the affects, but I have my kids near, a wonderful woman and lifelong companion, and I'm alive. In Jesus there is no fear, only hope. Hope that one day I can be completely healed. Until then I have found a constant source of peace.

Be strong and courageous. Do not be afraid; do not be discouraged, for the Lord your God will be with you wherever you go.
—Joshua 1:9 (English Standard Version)

EPILOGUE

Though our knowledge of PTSD is growing, it is still a misunderstood condition. There are a number of things that you can do to help yourself. There are also ways you can seek help from others.

- Do things to feel strong and safe in other parts of your life, such as exercising, eating well, and volunteering.
- Talk to a friend who has been through trauma or other hard times. A good friend who understands and cares is often the best medicine.
- Join a support group. It can help to be part of a group. Some groups focus on past memories. Others focus on the here and now. Still others focus on learning ways to relax.
- Talk to a professional. It may be helpful to talk to someone who is trained and experienced in dealing with PTSD. There are proven, effective treatments for PTSD. Your doctor can refer you to a therapist.
- Tell your family and friends about your PTSD. It can be helpful to talk to others as you try to place your long-ago experiences into perspective. It may also be helpful for others to know what may be the source of your anger, nerves, sleep, or memory problems. Then they can provide more support.

Don't be afraid to ask for help. Most of all try not to feel bad or embarrassed to ask for help. Asking for help when you need it is a sign of wisdom and strength.

"Don't worry about anything; instead, pray about everything. Tell God what you need, and thank him for all he has done. Then you will experience God's peace, which exceeds anything we can understand. His peace will guard your hearts and minds as you live in Christ Jesus" (Philippians 4:6-7 NIV).

CPSIA information can be obtained
at www.ICGtesting.com
Printed in the USA
FSOW02n2220280415
6780FS